Striker

 Clive Gifford

W

FRANKLIN WATTS
LONDON • SYDNEY

First published in 2006 by
Franklin Watts
338 Euston Road
London NW1 3BH

Franklin Watts Australia
Hachette Children's Books
Level 17/207 Kent Street
Sydney NSW 2015

Editor: Adrian Cole
Art Director: Jonathan Hair
Design: Matthew Lilly
Cover and design concept:
Peter Scoulding

Photograph credits:
AP/Topham: 6t; John Babb/Prosport/Topfoto: 3,
6b, 14; Mike Eason/Prosport/Topfoto: 7; Empics/
Topfoto: 8, 9, 10, 11, 12, 13, 15, 18, 19, 20, 24, 26, 27,
29; Tommy Hindley/Prosport/ Topfoto: 22, 23,
28; Maurice MacDonald/PA/ Topham: 17; PA/
Topham: 4, 20. 25; UPP/Topfoto: 16; Stephen
Wake/Prosport/ Topfoto: front cover.

A CIP catalogue record for this book is
available from the British Library.

Dewey classification: 796.334'2

ISBN-10: 0-7496-7039-8
ISBN-13: 978-0-7496-7039-9

Printed in China

Franklin Watts is a division of
Hachette Children's Books

Contents

The beautiful game

Football is an exciting, action-packed team sport. It is the most popular team sport in almost every country on Earth.

△ Pele (right) on the attack for Brazil. He once said of his football skills that, "everything is practice".

HALL OF FAME

Brazilian striker Pele (b.1940) scored 77 goals in the 91 games he played for his country. He scored over 1,280 goals throughout his career. He was the first person to describe football as "the beautiful game". Many people think he is the greatest striker ever seen.

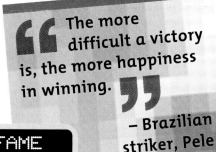

▷ Footballers dream of getting their hands on the football World Cup trophy.

Playing the game

In the full version of football, two teams have 11 players each. They play against each other in two, 45-minute halves. The aim is to use any part of the body, except the hands and arms, to get the ball into the other team's goal. It is only a goal if the ball completely crosses the goal line.

Attacking the goal

A football team works hard to get the ball. Then they move the ball towards the other side's goal. This is called attacking. The attacking team tries to pass the ball so their players can score a goal. Strikers score more than any other player because they play near the other team's goal.

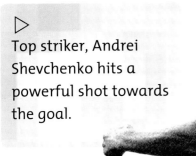

Top striker, Andrei Shevchenko hits a powerful shot towards the goal.

What is a striker?

A striker is a player whose main job is to score goals. Goals win games of football. This is why good strikers are very important.

An 11-player football team can have one, two or three strikers. Sometimes strikers run fast to get the ball. Other strikers are very skilled at running with the ball past defenders. A few strikers can jump well and score mostly with headers.

> " A football game without goals is like an afternoon without sunshine. "
>
> – Argentinian striker, Alfredo di Stéfano

▷ Tiffany Milbrett runs at Norway's defence. She is just 1.58m tall but a deadly striker who scored her 100th goal for the USA in 2005.

◁
Diego Maradona steps over the ball during a game in the 1986 World Cup.

HALL OF FAME

Diego Maradona was short, but very skilful. He scored 34 goals for Argentina. He also created goals for his team-mates using his amazing dribbling skills.

Birgit Prinz is Germany's leading goal scorer with over 80 goals for her country. She is a World Cup (2003) and European Championships (2005) winner with Germany.

All shapes and sizes

Some strikers are very tall. Peter Crouch and the Czech Republic's Jan Koller are over 2 metres tall. Other strikers are much shorter. Michael Owen is 1.72 metres and Diego Maradona 1.68 metres tall. Whatever their size, strikers always watch for a chance to score a goal.

It's best being a striker. If you miss five, then score the winner, you're a hero.

– Ian Rush, striker

Part of a team

A striker's goals can win a game, but a striker must play as part of a team. This means that the whole team works together to try and win the game.

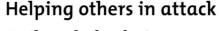

> **"** I've never considered one player to be all-important. In football you win or lose together as a team. **"**
>
> – Italian striker, Alessandro Del Piero

◁ Mia Hamm, striker for the USA, sprints to get away from an opponent and into space to receive the ball.

Helping others in attack

Strikers help their team-mates in attack by winning the ball and passing it to them. Strikers can also help by making an attacking run, which the other team's defenders try to stop by tackling them. This may leave space for one of the striker's team-mates to shoot at goal.

Defending from the front

When their team loses the ball, strikers can help their team-mates defend. They put themselves between the ball and their own goal. This makes it harder for the other side to get past and score a goal.

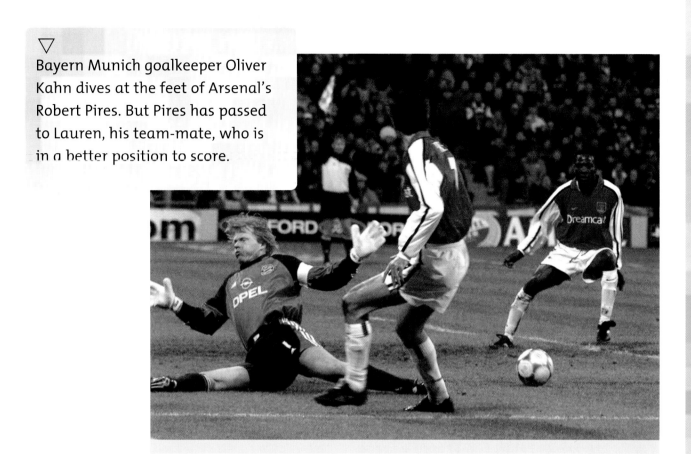

Bayern Munich goalkeeper Oliver Kahn dives at the feet of Arsenal's Robert Pires. But Pires has passed to Lauren, his team-mate, who is in a better position to score.

Unselfish play

Strikers love to score goals. But they must decide if a team-mate is better placed to score than themselves, and pass the ball to them. Strikers often work well together in pairs, called a strike partnership. Ronaldo and Raul, for example, formed a strike partnership at Spanish club, Real Madrid.

> I'm not obsessed with individual titles. I'm much more interested in being part of a team which wins trophies.
>
> – Brazil striker, Ronaldo

SKILLS TIPS

- As a striker, stay alert when your team is defending. You may be able to block a poor pass made by the other side and get the ball back.
- Keep your head up and watch the game. A sudden chance may come if you are the quickest to react.
- Never give up. Even if a game is hard work, you may get the chance to score or help a team-mate score.

In training

Before any training session or match, players warm up their bodies by jogging, sprinting and moving as they kick the ball. They also stretch the main muscles in their body. This helps to stop injuries.

> **I am building a fire, and everyday I train, I add more fuel. At just the right moment, I light the match.**
>
> – Mia Hamm, USA women's team striker

▷ HALL OF FAME

Mia Hamm is the leading goal scorer in women's football. She worked hard in training and during matches, and scored 158 goals for Team USA throughout her career.

Ronaldinho is famous for training and playing football with a smile on his face. The Brazilian was voted FIFA's World Footballer of the Year in both 2004 and 2005.

◁ Brazilian striker Ronaldo controls the ball during training before a World Cup Final.

Fast minds and feet

Strikers work to speed up their reactions in training. They may have footballs thrown to them at all different angles to practise their shooting, heading and ball control (see pages 14–15). Coaches and fitness trainers help them to improve their speed.

(Left to right) Wayne Rooney, Jamie Carragher and Frank Lampard perform a leg muscle stretch before training with England.

" Everything is practice. "

– Brazilian striker, Pele

Italy's Francesco Totti improves his agility by weaving between poles during training.

Strength and stamina

Strikers cannot simply wait for a chance to score. They have to work hard during a match. Stamina is the ability to run and work hard for a long time. Players improve their stamina with fitness training. Some players also build up extra strength in the gym.

Building skills

Strikers need to be good at shooting and heading. They must also be good at controlling the ball and passing. They work on these skills in match training.

SKILLS TIPS

- Practise controlling the ball with a friend. Ask them to throw the ball to you at different heights and speeds.
- Work on passing over long and short distances using both of your feet.
- Pass between friends but only allow each player to touch the ball twice. The first touch slows the ball down. The second touch is a pass.

Left or right foot?

Most footballers have a stronger foot that they pass or shoot with. Players should work really hard to improve their weaker foot. This makes a striker more dangerous because opponents don't know which foot they will use.

Brazilian striker Ronaldinho dribbles the ball past a defender. Dribbling is a skill. A player runs with the ball under control to get past the other team.

Ball control

Strikers learn how to slow a ball down with different parts of their body. This is called cushioning. They can use their chest, the top of their thigh and their foot to slow the ball down and drop it at their feet.

Shielding the ball

Sometimes, a striker has to protect the ball and keep it away from an opponent. They can put their body between the ball and their opponent. This is called shielding. They keep the ball under control before deciding what to do next.

⚠ Alan Shearer shields the ball well by putting his body between it and the defender.

15

Keeping in shape

Top strikers gain fame and fortune. But they must look after themselves and behave well on and off the football pitch.

Famous strikers, such as Ronaldo, Michael Owen and Ruud van Nistelrooy, are looked up to by many people, especially children. They have a responsibility to act well at all times. Top strikers are often asked to sign autographs and make appearances for charities.

▷

David Beckham signs an autograph. Top players like Beckham are in great demand from fans. Although he is a midfielder, Beckham scores lots of goals from free kicks.

Food for thought

Strikers stay fit by training hard and eating a healthy diet full of fresh fruit and vegetables. Some clubs give their players special diets to follow. They also weigh players and give them regular health checks.

Injuries and comebacks

Recovering from a serious injury is a worrying time for strikers. They fear losing their speed and goal-scoring skills. When a striker returns from injury, they often play practice and reserve games. These help them to rebuild their confidence.

▽ Ruud van Nistelrooy surges through towards the goal.

HALL OF FAME

Dutch striker Ruud van Nistelrooy suffered a serious knee injury in 2000. It took a year for him to make a successful comeback since when he has scored over 125 goals for Manchester United.

Brazilian striker Ronaldo returned from injury just before the 2002 World Cup. Yet, because he had trained hard, he was able to play well. He ended up as the leading scorer at the competition with eight goals.

" I know what it is like to have a long-term injury and I know I'm capable of working hard to be fit again. I'm obviously not happy about [the injury] but that's life and that's football. "

– Swedish striker, Henrik Larsson

Attacking play

Strikers are vital to a team's attacks. But they rely on their team-mates to make good passes from which they can try to score.

Crosses

A cross is a long pass made from the side of the pitch into the other team's penalty area. Most crosses are aimed high. This means they can be attacked by strikers with a header.

Scoring with a header

Strikers try to time their jump to meet the ball. They aim to get their head slightly above the ball. This allows them to head the ball downwards and towards the goal.

▽ South Korea's Ahn Jung-Hwan rises high to score a header against Italy.

Attacking attitude

Strikers rely on their team to make passes and crosses to them. A striker can repay his or her team's help by working hard and never giving up. Good fitness helps them chase down long passes or tackle a defender to win the ball.

△ Adriano, playing for his club Inter Milan, keeps his balance as he drives forward with the ball.

Scoring a goal

Scoring goals calls for a cool head and accurate finish. Strikers need to stay calm even when there are lots of other players around them.

Shoot to score

Shots can be hit really hard or more gently, but they must be on target. Strikers practise for many hours kicking the ball with their boot at different speeds. This helps them to make the perfect shot during a match.

> " You can get in all the greatest positions on the pitch, but if you panic when you get the ball, you won't score. Practising will help overcome this. "
>
> – England women's team striker, Amanda Barr

SKILLS TIPS

- When shooting, don't lean back. Try to keep your body over the ball. This helps keep the ball low and on target.
- Keep your eye on the ball.
- Concentrate on kicking and making good contact with the ball.
- Don't worry if you shoot and miss. Focus on what you are doing and get back into the game.

◁ Ronaldo scores against Manchester United in the Champions League with a powerful shot on target.

Staying alert

Strikers have to know what's going on around them in a match. They stay alert in case there is a sudden chance to attack. Some shots and headers bounce back off another player or the goalposts. The ball might come to a striker and give them a great chance to score.

Thierry Henry tries a spectacular overhead kick at goal.

Spectacular scoring

Some strikers are good at scoring spectacular goals. These include diving headers or cheeky chip shots, where the ball sails over the goalkeeper's head but dips down to land in the goal.

⚽ Talking tactics

The way a team plays and the exact roles of each player in a game are called a team's tactics.

> ❝ Football is a game you play with your brains. You have to be in the right place at the right moment, not too early, not too late. ❞
>
> – former Dutch international, Johan Cruyff

Formations

Teams line up in certain patterns of defenders, midfielders and strikers called formations. The 4-4-2 formation means that there are four defenders, four midfielders and two strikers. Teams use different formations in different games.

▷ HALL OF FAME

Ferenc Puskas was one of the finest ever attacking footballers. In 85 matches for Hungary, he scored an incredible 84 goals.

One of the most skilful of all strikers, Johan Cruyff scored 33 goals in 48 games for Holland. He was part of a Dutch team whose tactics saw players swap positions. It was known as 'total football'.

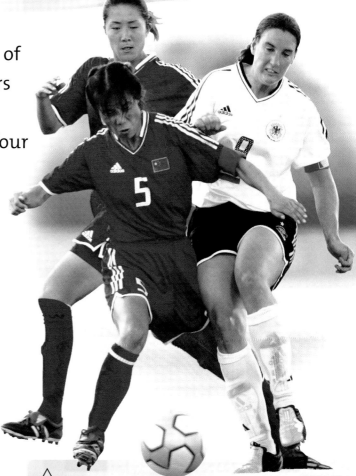

△ Germany's Birgit Prinz uses her strength to hold off Chinese opponents as she shoots. Prinz is sometimes used as a lone striker in a 4-5-1 formation.

Wingers

Some teams play with one or two attackers called wingers. These players tend to play near the sides of the pitch. Their aim is to cross the ball to a team-mate or to cut into the middle of the pitch to try and score themselves.

▷ Wayne Rooney sometimes plays out wide like a winger to receive the ball. He can then run at the other team's defence or make a good cross into the penalty area.

" From the age of 11, I went to Ajax and played every position apart from goalie...The experience of being a defender helps a striker to know how they think and how to beat them. "

– former Holland striker, Dennis Bergkamp

Strikers and substitutions

A substitution is where a player on the pitch is swapped for another player sitting on the substitutes bench. A manager or coach may substitute a striker with a defender or midfielder to help a team defend its lead.

Set pieces

Set pieces are situations such as corners, free kicks and penalties. They can offer a great chance for a striker to score or create a goal for a team-mate.

Free kicks

Free kicks are awarded by a referee when a foul has taken place. Some free kicks are near to the other side's goal and offer a good chance to score.

▷ Free kicks, like this one, can be bent around a defensive wall by kicking the ball so it spins and swerves.

Bending the ball

The defending team at a free kick often put a wall of players in front of their goal. Some strikers are very good at 'bending' the ball. They make it swerve around the side of the wall and towards the goal.

Taking a penalty

A penalty is taken from a spot less than 12 metres away from the goal line. Strikers often take penalties for their side. Some accurately pass the ball into one corner of the goal. Others prefer to kick the ball hard.

△
English striker James Beattie scores with a penalty hit low and into the corner.

⚽ Full time

Being a top striker is usually a short career. Strikers may be at their peak for only a few seasons. What do they do afterwards?

Retire or play on?

Today, most of the world's top male strikers are rich when they retire. Some, though, find it hard to give up the game. As a striker gets older, he may drop down a division or move to another country where the standard of football is lower. Most strikers retire by the time they reach 35.

> " The hardest part is what do you find to replace football – because there isn't anything. "
>
> – former England striker, Kevin Keegan

Jurgen Klinsmann passes on advice to young German striker, Mike Hanke.

Going into coaching

Many strikers take courses to become coaches. They may work at clubs as assistants and finally become the coach or manager of a club or national team. Retired German striker Jurgen Klinsmann was the head coach of Germany for the 2006 World Cup.

Staying in the game

Some players find other ways to stay in the game. They work as experts explaining a match or giving their views on TV, radio or in newspapers. Other ex-strikers work with young players at summer camps and football schools. Their hope is that one day they will discover a new goal-scoring star.

> " I want to stay in football, it's my passion, it's what I do best. "
>
> – Spanish international striker, Raul

△ Ex-England striker, Gary Lineker (left) was the top goalscorer at the 1986 World Cup. He is now a leading football presenter with BBC television.

 Websites

http://fifaworldcup.yahoo.com/o6/en
The official site of the 2006 World Cup held in Germany. It is packed with features and details of past and present World Cup tournaments.

http://www.bettersoccermorefun.com
A website full of useful and interesting coaching tips and tactics.

http://news.bbc.co.uk/sport1/hi/football/skills/default.stm#
This BBC website is packed full of skills and tips from top female and male players to improve your game as a striker.

http://www.shekicks.net
This excellent website offers in-depth coverage of women's football and contains lots of links to club and competition websites.

http://www.icons.com/home.html
Read the autobiographies and up to date newsletters of famous strikers, including Patrick Kluivert, Frederic Kanoute, Shola Ameobi at this website.

http://www.ifhof.com/hof/pele.asp
A detailed profile of Brazilian striker, Pele, at the International Football Hall of Fame website.

http://www.footballdatabase.com/site/home/index.php
A website packed with details on famous players, managers and competitions. A good place to head to find scoring records of famous strikers.

http://www.rsssf.com/miscellaneous/century.html
A webpage which if you scroll down reveals an updated list of the highest international goal scorers in football.

Every effort has been made by the Publishers to ensure that these websites contain no inappropriate or offensive material. However, because of the nature of the Internet, it is impossible to guarantee that the contents of these sites will not be altered. We strongly advise that Internet access is supervised by a responsible adult.

Glossary

Cross
– kicking the ball from the sideline to the centre of the pitch, usually into the other team's penalty area.

Dribbling
– moving the ball under close control with a series of kicks.

European Cup
– a competition played in by the best clubs in Europe. It is now known as the Champions League.

Formation
– the way a football team lines up to play a game.

Foul
– to break one of the rules of football.

Free kick
– a kick awarded to one team after a foul has been committed by the other team.

Interception
– when a player reaches an opponent's pass first.

Opponent
– a player from the team you are playing against.

Penalty
– a free kick given to the attacking team for a foul in the penalty area.

Penalty area
– the large rectangle marked on the pitch in front of the goal.

Professional
– being paid a wage to play football.

Referee
– the person on the pitch in charge of a game of football.

Set pieces
– free kicks, corners or penalties that involve movements practised in training.

Shielding
– placing your body, without fouling, between the ball and an opposition player.

Sideline
– one of the lines that marks the side of a football pitch.

Stamina
– the ability to run and work hard for long periods.

Substitution
– when one player is swapped with a different player on the same team.

Tackle
– using your feet to take the ball away from an opponent.

Tactics
– the different ways a team's players are told to play by their coach or manager to beat the other team.

Winger
– an attacker who plays near the edges of the pitch.

World Cup
– a competition, held every four years, for the best national teams in the world.

⚽ Index